M000017426

25 IDEAS TO CONNE

HEARTS, MINDS, AN

DON'T
JUST
TEACH...
REACH!

BY THOM & JOANI SCHULTZ

ND GROUP'S AMAZING TEAM OF CREATORS

Group
Real Bold Love.

DON'T JUST TEACH...REACH!

25 Ideas to Connect With Hearts, Minds, and Souls

Copyright © 2019 Group Publishing, Inc./ 0000 0001 0362 4853

Visit our website: **group.com**

All rights reserved. No part of this book may be reproduced in any manner whatsoever without prior written permission from the publisher. For information, visit group.com/permissions.

Credits
Authors: Thom and Joani Schultz
Contributors: Charity Kauffman, Mikal Keefer, and Rick Lawrence
Chief Creative Officer: Joani Schultz
Assistant Editor: Lyndsay Gerwing
Art Director & Design: Veronica Preston

Unless otherwise noted, scripture quotations are taken from the Holy Bible, New Living Translation, copyright ©1996, 2004, 2015 by Tyndale House Foundation. Used by permission of Tyndale House Publishers, Inc., Carol Stream, Illinois 60188. All rights reserved.

Scriptures taken from THE HOLY BIBLE, NEW INTERNATIONAL VERSION®, NIV® Copyright © 1973, 1978, 1984, 2010 by Biblica, Inc.™ Used by permission. All rights reserved worldwide.

Library of Congress Control Number: 2019943859

ISBN: 978-1-4707-6009-0
Printed in the United States of America.
10 9 8 7 6 5 4 3 2 1   28 27 26 25 24 23 22 21 20 19

TABLE OF CONTENTS

INTRODUCTION

A QUICK WORD ABOUT TEACHING...AND REACHING

You can tell when you're reaching others...

Whether you're teaching kids, teenagers, or adults, the signs are there. People are leaning in, soaking in every word. They're watching you closely. You can tell you're engaging something deep in them.

These are moments you're no longer teaching—you're *reaching*.

Reaching *hearts*...reaching *minds*...and reaching *souls*.

It doesn't get better than this. Not for you, and not for those you're leading.

You see, your job has never been to just teach. Your job—your calling—is to *reach* people with the good news that Jesus loves them and wants to be their friend.

And the 25 tips tucked in this little book will help you do that. They're the secret sauce of connecting more powerfully in your small group, Sunday school class, or youth group. They'll tell you what to do—and what to avoid doing.

Use them and you'll see boredom evaporate. Conversations will take a turn toward the significant. Faith and friendships will deepen as people grow closer to one another—and God—in fresh, surprising ways.

All because now you're *reaching*...not just teaching.

Happy reaching!

Thom & Joani

. . . .

"Show me the right path, O Lord; point out the road for me to follow. Lead me by your truth and teach me, for you are the God who saves me. All day long I put my hope in you."

(Psalm 25:4-5)

REACHING
HEARTS

" 'You must love the Lord your God with all your heart, all your soul, and all your mind.' This is the first and greatest commandment."

—*Jesus* (Matthew 22:37)

Denise is a preacher's kid. A *missionary* preacher's kid.

"But it wasn't until I was nearly 50 years old that I finally understood I was forgiven," she says. "It took that long before grace broke through to reach my heart."

And what unlocked that soul-soothing truth for Denise?

It wasn't one more sermon, that's for sure. Or reading one more Christian book. It happened when a woman leading a Bible study about grace set aside her teacher guide and engaged the group in conversation.

"She didn't settle for us being able to define what grace meant," remembers Denise. "She asked us each if we'd ever *experienced* grace. If we'd ever *felt* forgiven."

Denise had to admit: She hadn't.

That leader scuttled the rest of her lesson and gathered the rest of the group around Denise.

They accepted her, loved her, and helped her move past her guilt and shame and more fully into the joy of the Kingdom.

It took a leader who listened. A leader who didn't just *teach*...she *reached*.

And God moved though her to reach Denise's heart.

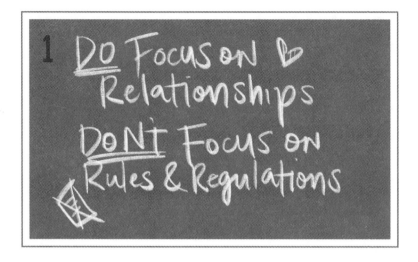

"I no longer call you servants, because a servant does not know his master's business. Instead, I have called you friends, for everything that I learned from my Father I have made known to you."

—*Jesus* (John 15:15, NIV)

- -

Jesus rattled his disciples.

They understood him calling them servants. But *friends*?

Yet here's Jesus, sharing that the relationship he wants isn't arm's-length respect but intimacy. He's after *friendship* with his followers—both then and now.

And being a friend is a very different deal from being a servant.

Servants serve because they don't have a choice. They show up out of obligation. And they live in fear of their masters.

Not so with friends. Friends show up because they want to be with you. They're eager to please you, not out of obligation but love. And they don't fear you; they trust you.

As you teach, how can you keep Jesus' desire to be friends front and center?

Here's how: Focus on relationships, not rules and regulations. Keep pointing back to Jesus' heart for us, his desire to have us be with him because we love him.

Build in time for relationships to flourish—with Jesus, with you, and with one another.

Always be moving toward friendship. That's where the good stuff is.

Because once the people you're teaching love Jesus, you won't have to convince them to live in a way that pleases Jesus. They'll naturally go straight there because that's how they'll please their friend.

HOW TO GET HERE?

"He [Jesus] asked his disciples, 'Who do people say that the Son of Man is?'

'Well,' they replied, 'some say John the Baptist, some say Elijah, and others say Jeremiah or one of the other prophets.'

Then he asked them, 'But who do you say I am?'"

(Matthew 16:13-15)

Jesus poses a question...waits...and lets everyone toss out an answer.

Smart move.

When people engage with a question by talking about it, what they discover sticks longer. They learn more. They grapple more deeply.

So if you want to reach others, give them the chance to talk. To think, process, and draw conclusions in real time.

And that means *everyone* gets to talk, not just a select few. Here's how:

To involve everyone, have people form pairs, and give partners time to chew on a question. Or form trios or even foursomes for discussions—and mix up ages if you can.

Just remember to switch up who's in pairs as you go. That way, members of your group get to know one another and hear fresh perspectives. Plus, nobody has to speak in front of the entire group.

After discussions, ask for a few report-backs, inviting people to share with the whole group what they talked about in pairs.

BONUS: As people get to know one another, they form friendships, which encourages them to return. They'll have close connections—and know they matter!

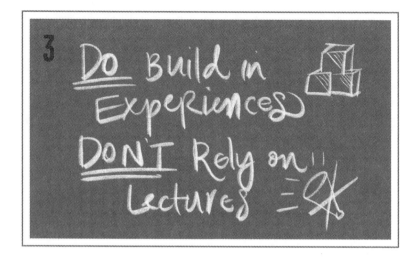

"So he [Jesus] got up from the table, took off his robe, wrapped a towel around his waist, and poured water into a basin. Then he began to wash the disciples' feet, drying them with the towel he had around him.

When Jesus came to Simon Peter, Peter said to him, 'Lord, are you going to wash my feet?'

Jesus replied, 'You don't understand now what I am doing, but someday you will.'"

(John 13:4-7)

. . . .

Peter learned more about servanthood—and Jesus—in that one moment than a lifetime of lectures would've taught him.

What you learn through experience seeps all the way down to your bones. It becomes bedrock in your life.

Think about a significant life lesson that has stuck with you a long time.

Did you learn that lesson through a speech or sermon? Did you read it in a book? Or was it something that happened to you?

Some educators report that learners retain up to *90 percent more* of what they experience than what they're told. That's especially true when you have learners talk about what they experienced.

If you want to reach people—to make lessons never-forget, change-your-life memorable—build in experiences and debriefing.

Instead of talking about the need for setting priorities, have people juggle balls in a group, representing everything they need to get done this week.

Share the story of Jonah while sitting inside the belly of a great fish, made out of a big taped-down black plastic sheet and a box fan.

Experiences *stick*—and sticky learning reaches people.

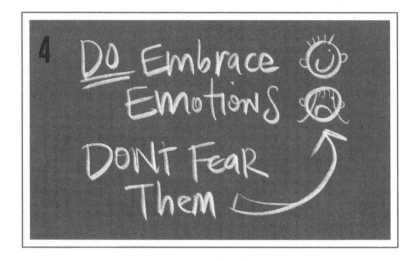

"One day Jesus said to his disciples, 'Let's cross to the other side of the lake.' So they got into a boat and started out... But soon a fierce storm came down on the lake. The boat was filling with water, and they were in real danger.

The disciples went and woke him [Jesus] up, shouting, 'Master, Master, we're going to drown!'

When Jesus woke up, he rebuked the wind and the raging waves. Suddenly the storm stopped and all was calm. Then he asked them, 'Where is your faith?'"

(Luke 8:22-25)

You know who isn't afraid of emotion when he's dealing with people?

Jesus.

The disciples are *terrified* when they awaken Jesus. And though he knows he's about to teach them a lesson about his power and love, Jesus doesn't first tell them to settle down and stop being upset.

Maybe Jesus knows what you'll discover as you move past teaching to experience reaching:

Emotion is an on-ramp to engagement. It's what opens up hearts and cements learning in place.

People who are engaged emotionally are wide awake and paying attention. When your class or group gets a little messy—people are grappling with ideas, interrupting one another, and not all quite in agreement—that's when *real* discovery is happening.

So don't squelch emotion; explore it.

Respectfully ask *why* someone's unsettled. Probe for what's *under* the emotion—it's a part of that person's story.

Some ways to gently probe include saying...

- "You seem to feel strongly about that. Help me understand why."
- "I'm wondering what's going on in you right now."

When emotion shows up while you're teaching, don't waste it.

Jesus didn't.

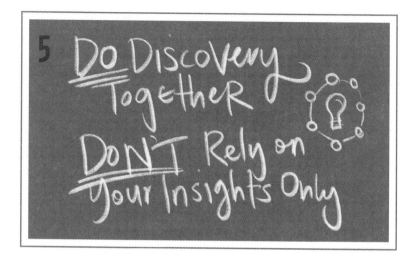

5 Do Discovery Together
Don't Rely on Your Insights Only

"The Kingdom of Heaven is like a treasure that a man discovered hidden in a field. In his excitement, he hid it again and sold everything he owned to get enough money to buy the field."

(Matthew 13:44)

. . . .

Anything we discover on our own has a special shine to it. We hold it close and feel as if it's ours because... well, *we* found it. *We* own it. And we're not about to let it go.

you're setting an expectation that God hasn't yet retired. You're declaring that God is still busy being God. You're embracing divine anticipation—the certainty that God will indeed show up.

So when you're teaching about God's love, don't settle for a nice story about it. Pause and ask how God has shown his love to someone in the room.

Then...wait.

Soon someone will give a real-life, real-time, real-personal example.

Ditto if you're teaching about God's patience, the Holy Spirit's leading, and practically any other topic.

Making space for God Sightings adds immediacy and excitement to your teaching that won't come any other way. That's because you're shifting the spotlight away from you onto God.

And you'll reach into the lives of people who share, giving them an opportunity to tell about God's righteousness.

Children, youth, and adults—they all have stories if you'll just ask.

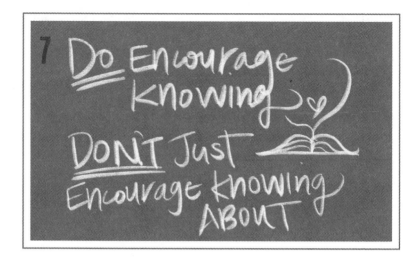

7 Do Encourage Knowing
Don't Just Encourage Knowing About

"On judgment day many will say to me, 'Lord! Lord! We prophesied in your name and cast out demons in your name and performed many miracles in your name.' But I will reply, 'I never knew you. Get away from me, you who break God's laws.'"

—*Jesus* (Matthew 7:22-23)

· ·

We love facts. They're clear and easy to talk about, and we can even ask about them to make sure people have been paying attention.

We like to know stuff—but studying facts about Jesus isn't how you go about falling in love with him. Or with people, either.

You didn't come to love a friend or spouse because you learned lots of facts about that person. You spent time together. Enjoyed each other. Laughed together. Discovered you can trust one another.

Then the love blossomed.

So don't worry too much about people mastering the material in your lessons. Being able to recite the Ten Commandments is less important than knowing the God who chiseled those commandments for Moses.

When you move people from knowing facts about Jesus to actually *knowing* him, they're in for a lot of joy. They find love. They choose to follow.

So emphasize transformation, not information.

8 Do Believe They'll Do It
DON'T Doubt They'll Do It

When you lead an experience, lead with enthusiasm and people will join in—even if you're afraid that one especially cranky person will think it's silly.

Two reasons: First, your enthusiasm is infectious—and you're also *doing* the experience as you lead, right?

And second, in our heart of hearts, we're all still 6 years old and want to play. We just never get the chance. Even when we're talking to and about Jesus, who invited us all to become like children.

The value of bringing experience into your classroom, small group, or youth group is so incredibly high that it's worth taking some risks.

Activities that might at first seem silly can change lives.

People in your group may never fully understand what it is to trust Jesus until they try a trust fall with a friend.

Lighting one tiny candle in a completely dark room is a vivid demonstration of how much light truth can shed.

If you believe your class or group will participate, they will. And when they then talk about what happened, they'll grow by leaps and bounds.

REACHING
MINDS

" 'You must love the Lord your God with all your heart, all your soul, and all your mind.' This is the first and greatest commandment."

—*Jesus* (Matthew 22:37)

Katrina fidgeted, not sure it was safe to tell two adults how she really felt about Sunday school. But they were asking, so she decided to be honest.

"It's boring," she said. "Too much like school."

Asked what they did at Sunday school, she replied, "We have to sit in chairs and memorize stuff."

Here's how the conversation went from there:

Us: What have you memorized?

Katrina: Verses from the Bible. We get a piece of candy if we come with verses memorized.

Us: Can you say the last verse you got some candy for?

Katrina: I don't remember.

Us: Do you remember any of them?

Katrina: No, I'm sorry.

Us: Well, can you remember what any of them mean?

Katrina: No. I guess I have a bad memory.

Us: Katrina, can you tell us what it takes for a person to get to heaven?

Katrina: Study hard.

If you'd been there to hear Katrina, you'd have heard her sigh as she realized that if you have to memorize your way into heaven, she's not going.

Katrina's teacher had been teaching—but not reaching.

You can do better.

"Jesus and his disciples left Galilee and went up to the villages near Caesarea Philippi. As they were walking along, he asked them, 'Who do people say I am?'"

(Mark 8:27)

· ·

Jesus loved pulling people in close by asking questions.

Questions like "Why do you doubt?" Like "Why worry about the speck in his eye when there's a log in your eye?" His questions engaged, enraged, enlightened—and changed lives.

People answering questions are often sorting out their answers in real time. They're doing more than processing *information*; they're deciding what they *believe*.

Questions help people own their faith and invite transformation.

So ask questions. But do as Jesus did and make those questions:

- **Open-ended.** Ask questions that can't be answered with a "yes" or "no" or by reciting a fact or answer people already know. Not "Where was Jesus born?" but "Why would Jesus be born in such a humble place?" (More about open-ended questions on page 54.)

- **Specific.** Answers to general questions reveal little. Don't ask, "What did Jesus say while on the cross?" but "Why did Jesus feel abandoned while on the cross?"

Making room for questions leaves less time for teacher talk—but that's a plus because people remember more of what they discuss than what they hear described.

A well-crafted question does more than teach. It reaches.

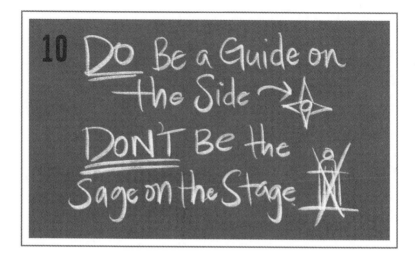

"He must become greater and greater, and I must become less and less."

(John 3:30)

· ·

If you're ever to go from teaching to reaching, that has to be your attitude, too.

It's not all about you or your communication skills.

Not about how clever the kids thought you were, how many laughs you got, or whether people applauded the show you pulled together.

Not about how many of your profound insights you shared or how many questions you were willing to answer.

It quite simply isn't about you. It's about how well you pointed people to Jesus at every opportunity and then stepped out of the way so they could see and hear from him.

Which means you're serving with humility. You're not the sage on the stage; you're a guide on the side.

A guide pointing straight to Jesus.

"His disciples came and asked him, 'Why do you use parables when you talk to the people?'"

(Matthew 13:10)

. . . .

When did we get so scared of silence?

Jesus didn't fear it. He told parables that he didn't explain, sending people home to quietly mull over what they heard—maybe forever.

Typical classroom teachers ask a question to promote participation but then wait, on average, less than 1.5 seconds before answering the questions *themselves*.

Don't do that. Instead, after you ask a question like "Why do you think Jesus told parables?" stay quiet.

Look around the room like you're expecting someone to speak up, and say...nothing.

Instead, count to 10.

Slowly.

Give others time to think. "Think time" leads to growth. Depth. Breakthroughs.

When you jump in too quickly, you rob others of the chance to grapple with their thoughts and emotions. You siphon opportunity for spiritual growth out of your teaching.

Pauses reach—so give them a place in your teaching.

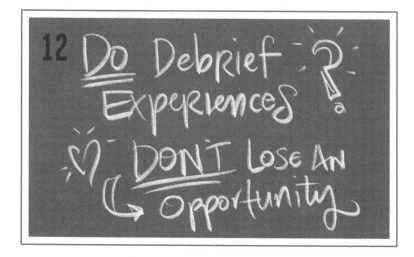

You want people to make the most of what they experience, so always build in debriefing.

That's where discovery happens. And discovery is the good stuff.

Discovery leads to life application that *sticks.*

Use three types of questions to give Jesus room to guide each person in how to live out a truth he's helped that person explore and own:

- **"How do you feel?"** questions help people get in touch with what they've just experienced.

- **"How is this like…?"** questions challenge people to make Scripture connections. Ask "How is what you just discovered like or unlike what [Jonah, Mary, Paul] discovered in the passage we read?"

- **"Now what?"** questions respectfully invite people to explore how their discoveries are relevant in their lives. How will those discoveries impact them moving forward?

Kids, adults, and teenagers are far likelier to do what *they* decide to do than what *you* decide they should try. So ask people what they want to do with what they've learned.

Ask…wait…and let them tell you.

"Each time he said, 'My grace is all you need. My power works best in weakness.' So now I am glad to boast about my weaknesses, so that the power of Christ can work through me."

(2 Corinthians 12:9)

If Paul was hoping to prompt his readers to share their own stories of weaknesses, he went about it the right way.

He shared first.

You can't expect people in your group to risk being vulnerable until you've been vulnerable first. Practically speaking, that means you also answer digging-deeper questions you toss at your group.

If you say, "Tell about a time you were hurt," start by sharing your own story of pain. If you ask, "When do you find it hard to trust God?" share a time like that you keep revisiting.

You're modeling vulnerability and setting the bar for the kind of sharing you want to have happen in the group. You're helping people get to know—and trust—you and see how Jesus is real to you.

And here's a secret: *You go first.*

Don't make people wait to see if it's safe—your sharing *makes* it safe.

> **"Therefore, accept each other just as Christ has accepted you so that God will be given glory."**
>
> (Romans 15:7)

Here's the thing about acceptance: You can accept someone's thoughts without agreeing with those thoughts. That's key if you want to reach imperfect people.

People like…well, like you.

This concept is so freeing, so true, so able to help you reach as you teach that it alone is worth the price of admission.

So here it is again: *You can accept someone's thoughts without endorsing those thoughts.* And carry it even further: *You can accept a person without endorsing everything that person believes.*

So do for others what Jesus is doing for you: Offer acceptance and friendship. And if someone believes something untrue, respectfully help the person rethink that belief by continuing the conversation with phrases like these:

"I'm wondering how you came to that conclusion."

"It's been my experience that..."

"As for me, I've discovered..."

"Tell me more..."

Judgment shuts down discovery and relationship. Acceptance leaves the doors open and doesn't compromise your integrity.

So don't judge. Instead, accept—and see where Jesus takes it from there.

"*Acceptance* does not mean *endorsement.* When we confuse the two, we destroy the very space God wants to work in."

—Doug Pollock (*God Space*)

"One of the twelve disciples, Thomas (nicknamed the Twin), was not with the others when Jesus came. They told him, 'We have seen the Lord!'

But he replied, 'I won't believe it unless I see the nail wounds in his hands, put my fingers into them, and place my hand into the wound in his side.'"

(John 20:24-25)

. . . .

Jesus appears, Thomas gets the proof he needs, and somewhere along the line he's saddled with a new nickname: "Doubting Thomas."

But we could as easily call him "Transparent Thomas." He has doubts, he says so, and Jesus meets him at those doubts and resolves them. What Jesus *doesn't* do is condemn or ridicule Thomas.

Unlike what some teachers do when a hand shoots skyward and someone says, "Yes, but how do I know that's really *true*?"

If people can't raise doubts about their faith in church, where can they talk about those doubts? And what sort of information will they get elsewhere?

We sometimes shut down doubts because, secretly, we share them. And because doubts are generally about hard stuff—stuff we can't explain or don't really understand ourselves.

When a sincere doubt surfaces, hear it. Sum it up so you're sure you understand. Then invite a conversation; maybe someone else in the room can speak to the issue.

And have these words ready: "I don't know. But together let's explore that." WONDER WALL

Make your class or group a safe place for doubts. Take them—and your doubters—seriously. We all doubt at times. We're all in this together.

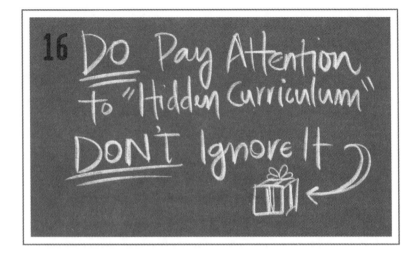

16 DO Pay Attention to "Hidden Curriculum" DON'T Ignore It

Reaching focuses less on what you're *teaching* and more on what they're *learning*.

They aren't always the same.

Think of it as "hidden curriculum." It's the stuff your learners learn that you don't necessarily *plan* for them to learn but they pick up through the experience.

- **If you use lots of complicated theological words** while talking about God, learners decide knowing God must be complicated, too. They think God's central message for them can't be as simple as "I love you and want to be your friend; come to me."

- **If you insist people memorize material,** you're signaling that what God cares about most is what they tuck away temporarily into short-term memory.

- **If you fail to learn or use people's names,** you're leading them to believe you see them as a herd, not individuals...so you must not care all that much.

- **If you pack Bible lessons with puzzles,** mazes, fill-in-the-blanks, and word searches and scrambles, you're saying the Bible—and God—are confusing and intentionally elusive.

But if you're welcoming and caring, they assume the Jesus you're representing is, too. If you invite and listen to their concerns, they're quick to believe they matter. If you pause to pray for them, they learn God is always accessible and interested.

What you do and how you do it speaks volumes—sometimes louder than anything else.

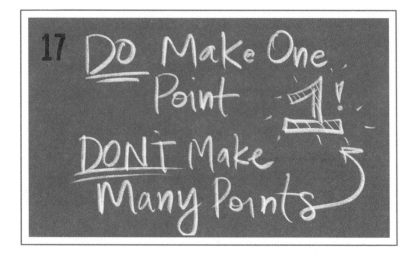

"There is so much more I want to tell you, but you can't bear it now."

(John 16:12)

. . . .

Your teaching will be far stronger if in every lesson, you have just one point you want people to carry away with them. One central truth you want to see settle into their hearts, minds, and souls.

So pick one point you want to communicate, write it on a sticky note, and keep that note in view as you prepare your next lesson.

Be sure everything you say and do points back to that central truth.

If you use a conversation starter, be sure it starts a conversation about that truth.

If you add a game, make it one that can be debriefed to reinforce that truth.

Every Bible passage, craft, illustration, song, reading, journaling exercise, snack, and talking point earns its place by exploring the one truth written on that sticky note in front of you.

Ask yourself: Would you rather make one point that sticks or 27 that don't?

Try to do too much in a lesson and you end up accomplishing nothing.

Less is more.

When you have the discipline to do less, you move past teaching and end up reaching.

yes!

INCREASE YOUR LESSON'S STICKINESS
by doing these things:

 PICK ONE CENTRAL POINT and come back to it often. Repeat it. Reinforce it. Refer to it using a variety of learning styles.

 TELL STORIES that support your one point. Stories stick longer than lectures, especially if you engage the imaginations of learners through active participation on their part.

 USE ANALOGIES. It's easier to remember new things if they build on the familiar. Build on existing foundations for sturdy, ongoing understanding.

 GIVE EXAMPLES. Examples make the theoretical concrete and help inspire personal application.

 PROVIDE SIMPLE, COMPELLING, MEMORABLE VISUALS that reinforce your point. Just make sure the visuals actually illustrate the point; visuals for the sake of visuals are a distraction.

SAY IT AGAIN—but slightly different each time. People recall with greater clarity connections they make themselves, so give them ample opportunities to make those discoveries.

BUILD IN REFLECTION, giving listeners time to consider what they've learned in your lesson and why it matters.

REVIEW WHAT WAS COVERED at the end of the lesson, and if possible, keep reviewing from lesson to lesson. Seldom is one exposure to material enough to make it truly memorable.

ENCOURAGE LEARNERS TO SUMMARIZE what the've heard. Asking learners to restate your main points in their own words helps you confirm you were understood.

BETTER YET, DON'T RELY JUST ON THE POWER OF YOUR WORDS. Build in a "pair discussion" to talk about your point. Ask questions. Add an experience using the tips you'll find in this guide.

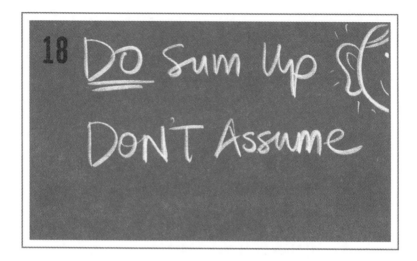

> **"Fools have no interest in understanding; they only want to air their own opinions."**
>
> (Proverbs 18:2)

. . . .

Here's how to be sure you'll never head down that path: Master the art of reflective listening, the art of summing up before you carry conversations further.

It's not hard, but it does require discipline and a desire to seek understanding.

Imagine that someone has just delivered a monologue about why she thinks Jesus is a nice guy but not God's Son, and certainly not the only way to heaven.

Don't leap in to set her straight.

Instead, sum up what you heard her say. Not every word, but the major concepts. If you get it right, she'll know she was understood. If you missed something significant, she'll tell you.

Maybe "I hear you saying you have a lot of respect for Jesus, but you're not sure he's divine. And certainly not the only way to get to heaven."

Once you sum up, you can either ask a follow-up question or check to see if she's willing to hear your take on the topic at hand.

You're signaling respect. You're not assuming you understand; by summing up you're making sure.

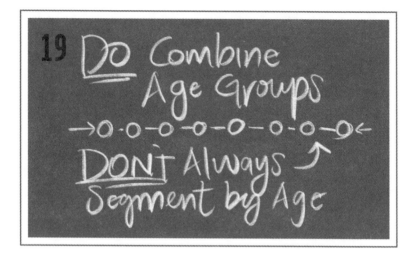

Grouping learners strictly by age assumes everyone develops at the same rate, learns at the same pace, and has similar needs and interests.

Faulty assumption.

Broad categories make sense—adults and first-graders aren't on remotely the same page—but consider creating mixed-age groups within elementary students or teenagers. And the Newlyweds and Senior Saints groups have more to talk about than you might first assume.

Mixing things up unleashes the power of multi-age learning in lots of ways:

- **Learning is enhanced** as people move at their own pace. There's less pressure to keep pace with peers. And older ones often tutor younger ones, who love the extra attention.

- **Cooperation skills are sharpened** as everyone looks out for one another.

- **You get flexibility** because you can form as many mixed-age groups as you need. No worries if few third-graders show and the fifth-grade group is twice its usual size.

- **Discipline problems largely disappear.** You can separate ages that bring out the worst in each other. For example, those fifth-grade boys won't all be trying to impress one another.

Try mixing things up as an experiment. Give it a month, and see how it works for you. (Spoiler alert: It will be *great*!)

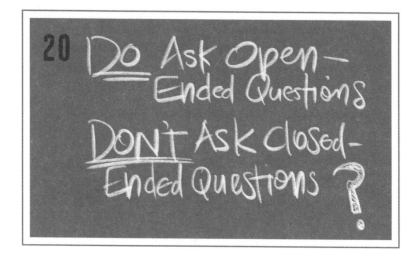

"One day an expert in religious law stood up to test Jesus by asking him this question: 'Teacher, what should I do to inherit eternal life?'

Jesus replied, 'What does the law of Moses say? How do you read it?'"

(Luke 10:25-26)

. . . .

Open-ended questions open doors. Closed-ended questions shut them.

Teachers tend to ask closed-ended questions.

"What tribe is Paul from?" (Benjamin)

"In which river was Jesus baptized?" (Jordan)

"How many angels can dance on the head of a pin?" (Um...uh...)

Not much room for discussion with closed-ended questions. Either you know the answer or you don't. They're designed to help you feel smart or...not.

Open-ended questions can't be answered with a factoid or a simple "yes" or "no." They're engaging. They require thought and invite conversation. They reach.

"Why do you call me good?" (Jesus asked that in Luke 18:19.)

"Why are you afraid?" (Jesus again in Matthew 8:26.)

"Why did you doubt me?" (Guess who—in Matthew 14:31.)

If you want to reach minds, use open-ended questions. You're guaranteed to get everyone engaged and thinking.

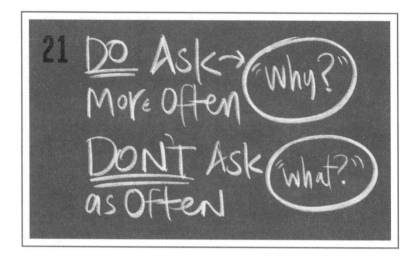

21 DO Ask ←→ "Why?"
More Often
DON'T Ask "what?"
as Often

"Someone came to Jesus with this question: 'Teacher, what good deed must I do to have eternal life?'

'Why ask me about what is good?' Jesus replied."

(Matthew 19:16-17)

· ·

"Why?" questions rock us back on our heels. They quietly demand that we consider our motives. Explain our thinking. Reconsider our conclusion and positions.

You'll be amazed at how quickly "Why?" questions help you reach minds as well as hearts—especially if you stack a few "Why?" questions on top of each other.

You: Why do you think Jesus didn't just give this guy an answer?

Student: Maybe because he wanted the guy to think for himself.

You: Why would Jesus want someone to think for himself?

Student: Because then he has to make a choice. He has to decide.

You: Why would Jesus want someone to make decisions?

Student: Because then the guy could decide to be with Jesus.

Bingo.

But equally important is reducing your "What?" questions. They review material but seldom lead anywhere.

You: What did the man ask Jesus?

Student: He asked about doing a good deed.

You: What did Jesus say to the guy?

Student: He asked why the guy was asking Jesus about being good.

You: Okay, I guess you read the lesson.

If you're after more than that—and you are—then **ask way more "Why?" questions than "What?" questions.**

REACHING SOULS

" 'You must love the Lord your God with all your heart, all your soul, and all your mind.' This is the first and greatest commandment."

—*Jesus* (Matthew 22:37)

Nicole showed up in Cal's teen group about six months ago, invited by a friend.

"She wasn't raised in the church," says Cal. "At first she didn't say much. She thought all the other kids knew more than she knew, had families far more focused on church and God than hers.

"She didn't think she belonged, but she felt drawn to the group."

But Nicole does something that has made the group far richer for everyone in it.

"She asks incredible questions," says Cal.

Cal remembers the night the group was talking about loving enemies when Nicole asked, "What if I *act* loving toward an enemy but I don't *feel* loving? Does that count?"

Which gets at the very heart of what Jesus was talking about.

Cal paused and said to her, "Nicole, you ask the questions everyone's thinking but won't ask. That's just amazing."

Cal remembers seeing a shift in Nicole's whole countenance. What she'd considered a weakness—that she didn't know a lot—was actually a strength. She *did* belong. She *did* contribute. She *did* have value.

"It was like watching a balloon inflate," says Cal. "You could see the light come into her eyes."

Cal—and the entire group—had touched the very essence of who Nicole was, her very identity. They'd reached her soul because they'd seen her, valued her, and affirmed her.

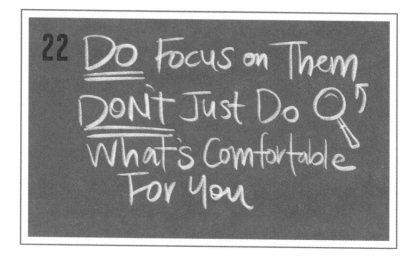

22 Do Focus on Them Don't Just Do What's Comfortable For You

There are multiple ways to learn—and your lessons will be stronger if you incorporate more than one method or style.

Here's the problem: Most of us tend to teach the same way we learn. That means if you're a lecture lover, you teach using lectures. If you're an artist, your lessons always include drawing or dance.

We end up talking one language even though there are people with us who don't necessarily speak that same language.

We've provided a quick chart of eight learning styles— eight ways to be "smart"—on pages 64-65.

Glance at it and you'll easily be able to pick out a few styles that reflect how you're wired.

So do this: Pick a learning style that's clearly not yours. Pick a couple. Then as you prepare your next lesson, work in an activity that reflects that style.

A graph for the visual learners. A chance to get up and do something for your kinesthetic learners. You'll see lightbulbs flash on over the heads of people who don't pay close attention when you lecture.

Just make sure everything you do ties to the point of your lesson.

No tossing in stuff for the sake of tossing it in.

SMART CHART
8 Ways Your Learners Learn Best

from Howard Gardner's multiple intelligences theory

Whether you're teaching children, youth, or adults, your learners are wired to take in and process information in a variety of ways. Here are the most common:

WORD SMART

Strengths: Reasoning, public speaking, debate, listening, writing

Use words—verbal or written—to reach these learners. Have discussions, read or tell stories, or write in journals.

PICTURE SMART

Strengths: Artistic, imaginative, adept with metaphors

Use pictures, images, and spatial understanding to reach these learners. View diagrams and videos, create arts and crafts, or doodle and draw.

MUSIC SMART

Strengths: Emotionally tuned to music, rhythm, pitch

Use sound and music to connect. Sing, play music, listen to music, or learn content by setting it to music.

BODY SMART

Strengths: Athletic, good at crafts, enjoy active learning

Both experience and sense of touch light up these learners. Use physical movement and games, have them act out stories, or let people fiddle with objects as they listen.

LOGIC SMART

Strengths: Abstract thinkers, organized, adept problem-solvers

Logic and reasoning are the welcome mats out front for these learners. Have people solve problems, explore, or ask and answer probing questions.

PEOPLE SMART

Strengths: Cooperative, intuitive, understanding, friendly

Group interaction is how to reach these learners. They're drawn to get-acquainted activities, discussion and debriefing, group service activities, and social times.

SELF SMART

Strengths: Self-aware, reflective, self-motivated

These learners enjoy self-study. They take in information through independent study, prayer, meditation, and quiet times.

NATURE SMART

Strengths: Environmentally aware, observant, like the outdoors and animals

These learners love being outside taking walks, tending to natural resources, and collecting and classifying elements of the natural world.

23 Do Listen Carefully. Don't overlook Listening

You can't reach people who aren't sure you notice them.

And if you're plowing through a lesson without paying much attention to them, they're pretty sure you haven't noticed they're in the room.

- When someone raises a hand to ask a question and you don't respond.

- When someone says, "I'm not sure I agree with that," and you blow on past without exploring what was said.

- When someone is clearly upset by something that was said or done, and you pretend to not see it rather than stop and respond.

It looks from where they sit that you don't care. **And if they aren't sure you care about them, they won't care what you have to say.**

So, do this: *Listen lavishly.* Nothing signals that you care like listening.

Here's how to do it:

- Look up. Know your lesson well enough that you're making eye contact and can see what's happening in the room.

- When you're challenged, turn off that inner voice that's preparing a rebuttal, and sum up what you heard said instead. It proves you're paying attention.

- Look like you're listening; listen with your whole body, not just your ears.

LISTENING WITH YOUR WHOLE BODY

Here's how to signal that you're listening:

- **Relax** so the person speaking will relax, too.
- **Open up your body language**—arms open and not crossed, head up.
- **Lean in** to send the message you're interested.

- **Eye contact**—without staring, maintain eye contact.
- **Sit or stand comfortably** and at the same eye level as the person talking.
- **Pocket your phone**—even having it visible nearby is a distraction.

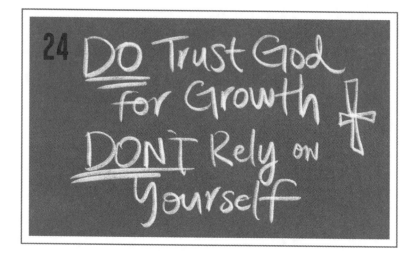

24 DO Trust God for Growth DON'T Rely on Yourself

"I planted the seed in your hearts, and Apollos watered it, but it was God who made it grow. It's not important who does the planting, or who does the watering. What's important is that God makes the seed grow."

(1 Corinthians 3:6-7)

. . . .

As a teacher and leader, here's a good thing to remember:

It's *God's* job to cause growth. It's *our* job to till the soil and faithfully plant what's true and loving in the lives of those we serve.

We plant. We water.

But it's God who causes growth, and when we step into his shoes, we quickly find we're ill-prepared to be there.

Here's how you till soil and plant seeds:

- **Pray for those you teach.** Ask them how they'd like you to pray for them, and ask Jesus how he'd have you pray, too.

- **Care and let them know you care.** You do that by learning their names, asking follow-up questions, and remembering previous conversations.

- **Be authentic.** You're not perfect, either, and they know that. They're just not sure you know it unless you tell them. It's okay to admit mistakes.

- **Keep pointing people to Jesus.** When your words and deeds help people see, love, and follow Jesus, you're planting seeds.

God will nurture those seeds into a bountiful harvest.

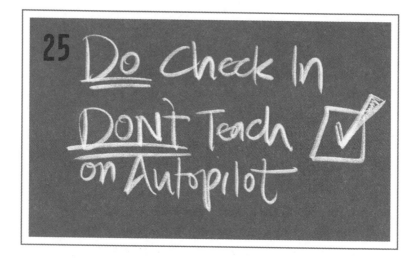

25 Do Check In DON'T Teach on Autopilot ✓

How do you know if people are really growing spiritually? if you're making a difference? if something needs to change so learning sticks?

Here are nine ways to assess understanding, retention, and application:

- **Observation:** Watch people's behavior for examples of learned lessons.

- **Verbal responses:** Ask what people have learned, right after a lesson and in a few weeks. The tips in this book help learners remember more, longer.

- **Written records:** Prayer journals, letters, class newsletters—check learning by reading what they write.

- **In-class videos:** Ask small groups to create an instant video that shows what they've learned, and watch their efforts together in class.

- **Drawing:** Have everyone sketch Bible stories, draw murals, or create cartoon strips that demonstrate what they've learned.

- **Projects:** Ask them to create—and then do—practical projects that put what they've learned into action.

- **Personal storytelling:** Give people space to talk about how they're growing. Help them explore what God is doing in and through them.

- **Faith histories:** Have people chronicle their faith histories through photos, important dates and events, and letters from people who've seen them grow spiritually.

- **Verse explanations:** Ask people to explain a Bible passage as if to a very young child. Ask learners to include what the passage means to them personally.

What You Do Matters

"Every time I think of you, I give thanks to my God. Whenever I pray, I make my requests for all of you with joy, for you have been my partners in spreading the Good News about Christ from the time you first heard it until now. And I am certain that God, who began the good work within you, will continue his work until it is finally finished on the day when Christ Jesus returns."

(Philippians 1:3-6)

. . . .

As you lead others deeper into a friendship with God, you're doing more than just teaching.

You're *reaching*.

Reaching hearts...minds...and souls.

You're planting seeds that God will one day transform into a bountiful harvest.

We're praying for you—and for the lives you touch.

God bless you.